Aberdeenshire

COUNCIL

Aberdeenshire Libraries
www.aberdeenshire.gov.uk/libraries
Renewals Hotline 01224 661511

Harman, Alice

FACT CAT

NORTHERN IRELAND

Alice Harman

WAYLAND

FACT CAT

Get your paws on this fantastic new mega-series from Wayland!

Join our Fact Cat on a journey of fun learning about every subject under the sun!

First published in 2014 by Wayland
© Wayland 2014

Wayland
Hachette Children's Books
338 Euston Road
London NW1 3BH

Wayland Australia
Level 17/207 Kent Street
Sydney NSW 2000

Produced for Wayland by
White-Thomson Publishing Ltd
www.wtpub.co.uk
+44 (0) 843 208 7460

Editor: Alice Harman
Design: Rocket Design (East Anglia) Ltd
Fact Cat illustrations: Shutterstock/Julien Troneur
Other illustrations: Stefan Chabluk
Consultant: Kate Ruttle

A catalogue for this title is available from the British Library

ISBN: 978 0 7502 8440 0
ebook ISBN: 978 0 7502 8733 3

Dewey Number: 914.1'6-dc23

10 9 8 7 6 5 4 3 2 1

Wayland is a division of Hachette Children's Books,
an Hachette UK company.
www.hachette.co.uk

Printed and bound in China

Picture and illustration credits:
Alamy: DWImages Northern Ireland 6, Simon Reddy 13, AF archive 18; Belfast City Council: 12; Chabluk, Stefan: 4; Corbis: Colin McPherson 19; Dreamstime: Roman Zaremba 5, Ian Whitworth 8, Tonybrindley 17; Getty: VI-Images 20; Library of Congress: 11; NASA: 19 background; Northern Ireland Tourist Board: 9, 16, 21; Shutterstock: Paco Lonzano 7, Louise Cukrov 10, Pecold 14, Jane McIlroy 15, Paul Krugman cover, nazlisart cover flag.

Every effort has been made to clear copyright. Should there be any inadvertent omission, please apply to the publisher for rectification.

The author, Alice Harman, is a writer and editor specialising in children's educational publishing.

The consultant, Kate Ruttle, is a literacy expert and SENCO, and teaches in Suffolk.

FACT CAT FACT

There is a question for you to answer on each spread in this book. You can check your answers on page 24.

CONTENTS

WELCOME TU NORTHERN IRELAND

Northern Ireland is part of the United Kingdom, which is also called the UK. The other countries in the UK are Scotland, England and Wales.

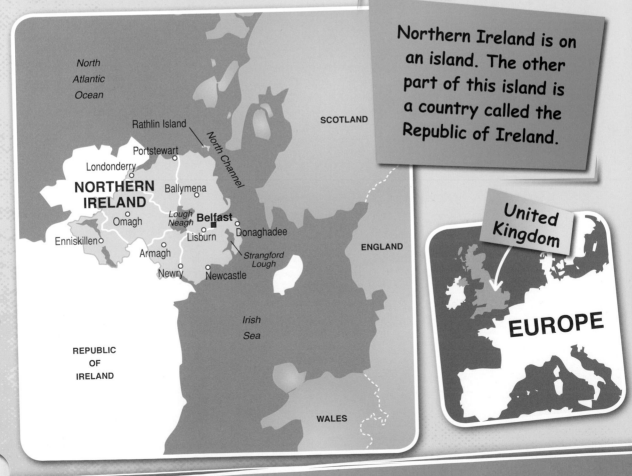

Northern Ireland is on an island. The other part of this island is a country called the Republic of Ireland.

North Atlantic Ocean

SCOTLAND

Rathlin Island

North Channel

Portstewart

Londonderry

NORTHERN IRELAND

Ballymena

Omagh

Lough Neagh

Belfast

Lisburn

Donaghadee

Enniskillen

Strangford Lough

ENGLAND

Armagh

Newry

Newcastle

Irish Sea

REPUBLIC OF IRELAND

United Kingdom

EUROPE

WALES

Belfast is the **capital** city of Northern Ireland. It is the largest city in the country, and around 280,000 people live there. It is built beside the sea.

Belfast Castle is built on a tall hill above the city. Find out why part of this hill is called 'Napoleon's Nose'.

FACT CAT FACT

An old story says that Belfast Castle is only safe from trouble if a white cat lives at the castle. A 'Cat Garden' next to the castle has nine cats made of stone, metal and plants.

CITIES

There are five cities in Northern Ireland. They are Belfast, Lisburn, Londonderry, Armagh and Newry. Armagh is one of the UK's smallest cities, with around 15,000 people living there.

Northern Ireland is split into six areas called counties. The city of Armagh (pictured below) is in County Armagh. Find out the names of the other counties.

Londonderry is the second-largest city in Northern Ireland. It is often called Derry. It is in the north-west of the country, very close to the Republic of Ireland.

Londonderry's city walls were built around 400 years ago. People used the cannons to help defend the city from attackers.

FACT CAT FACT

During a war around 325 years ago, English soldiers tried to take over Londonderry. They attacked the city for 105 days, but they never got past the great walls.

THE COAST

Northern Ireland has a long, rocky coast with many tall **cliffs**. There are long, sandy beaches, and **shingle** beaches made of small stones.

White Park Bay is on the north coast. Wild flowers and butterflies live in the grassy area behind the beach. Find out one type of butterfly that can be seen there.

Many people live in towns and villages along the coast of Northern Ireland. **Tourists** often like to visit seaside towns such as Portstewart, Newcastle and Donaghadee.

crabs

Fishermen in Donaghadee catch many types of fish. They also catch other sea creatures such as crabs and lobsters.

FACT CAT **FACT**

The biggest lobster ever caught in Northern Ireland weighed more than 5 kg (11 lbs). That is the same weight as two cats!

HISTORY

Until around 20 years ago, there was a lot of fighting in Northern Ireland. Some people wanted the country to be part of the UK, and others thought it should be part of the Republic of Ireland.

Belfast has lots of famous **murals** painted on buildings. This one is about children growing up in a peaceful Northern Ireland, with no fighting.

NO MORE

No more bombing no more murder
No more killing of our sons
No more standing at the grave side
Having to bury our loved ones

No more waiting up every hour
Hoping our children, they come home
No more maimed or wounded people
Who have suffered all alone

No more minutes to leave a building
No more fear of just parked cars
No more looking over our shoulders
No more killing in our bars

No more hatred from our children
No more. No more. No more !

The *Titanic* is one of the most famous ships in history, and it was built in Belfast. It sank on its first trip to the USA, and more than 1500 people died.

Some of the richest people in the world travelled on the *Titanic*. The huge ship had a library, a gym, a swimming pool and six restaurants and cafés.

The *Titanic* was built around 100 years ago. Many other great ships were made in Belfast. Can you find out the name of one of them?

FOOD

Many towns and villages in Northern Ireland still have butcher's shops, bakeries and farm shops run by families. These shops sell fresh food that is made or grown in the area.

Lots of farmers sell food at St George's Market in Belfast. People come to buy bread, meat, fruit, vegetables and cheese.

Northern Ireland's **traditional** dishes often include potato or bread. Potato farl is a type of bread made from potato. People also eat meat **stews**, sausages and **pasties**.

An Ulster Fry (pictured below) is a type of Northern Irish breakfast. Try to find a recipe for soda bread. Ask an adult to help you make it!

soda bread

potato farl

black pudding

FACT CAT FACT

Dulse is a salty, crispy snack food made of **seaweed**. Fishermen used to bring in the seaweed to sell, so they could earn a bit more money.

SIGHTS

The Giant's Causeway is a **rock formation** on the north-east coast. It is made of 40,000 **columns** of rock. It was created 50 million years ago by **lava** from a **volcano**.

Around 600,000 people visit the Giant's Causeway every year.

FACT CAT FACT

An old story says that a magical giant called Finn McCool built the Giant's Causeway so he could step over the sea to Scotland without getting his feet wet!

Northern Ireland has many stone buildings and **monuments** that were created hundreds or thousands of years ago. Tourists visit these towers, castles, churches and other places.

These stones are part of the Ballymacdermot Court Tomb. Important people were buried here when they died. Can you find out when the tomb was built?

WILDLIFE

Northern Ireland has many types of **habitat**, where different animals like to live. There are lizards in grassy areas, deer and **hares** in the forest, and **otters** by the rivers.

Seals live along the coast, on islands and in large **lakes**. Find out which types of seal live in Strangford Lough, one of Northern Ireland's biggest lakes.

In the summer, more than 250,000 puffins live on the rocky coast of Rathlin Island. Puffins spend most of the year in the sea, often very far from land.

More than 400 types of birds live in Northern Ireland. **Birds of prey** such as peregrine falcons and red kites hunt in fields for mice. Sea birds dive into the water to catch fish.

FACT CAT FACT

Puffins say goodbye to each other by rubbing and hitting their **beaks** together. This is called beaking.

FAMOUS PEOPLE

There are lots of great writers, actors and musicians from Northern Ireland. One famous writer is C. S. Lewis. He wrote the *Chronicles of Narnia* books, set in the magical world of Narnia.

FACT CAT FACT

C. S. Lewis said that Northern Ireland's Mourne Mountains helped him to imagine Narnia. He thought they looked as if a giant might live there!

The Lion, the Witch and the Wardrobe is C. S. Lewis's most famous book. Can you find out the name of another book set in Narnia?

Jocelyn Bell Burnell is a Northern Irish scientist who studies outer space. She helped to discover a type of star called a pulsar. She has won many awards for her work.

In 2014, Jocelyn Bell Burnell was the first woman ever to become president of the Royal Society. This is a very famous group of scientists.

SPORT

Some of the most popular sports in Northern Ireland are football, rugby, **hockey** and **cricket**. People enjoy watching and playing these sports.

There are 50 women's football teams playing in Northern Ireland. Top players also make up the Northern Ireland team in **international** games.

FACT CAT FACT

Tony McCoy is a very famous horse-racing **jockey** from Northern Ireland. He has won more than 4000 races, and is one of the best jockeys of all time.

Gaelic Games are traditional Irish sports that include Gaelic football, hurling, Gaelic handball and rounders. Gaelic football players can kick, throw, carry and bounce the ball.

Hurling is one of the fastest ball games in the world. Can you find out when people first played it?

QUIZ

Try to answer the questions below. Look back through the book to help you. Check your answers on page 24.

1 What material is the Giant's Causeway made of?

a) wood

b) metal

c) rock

2 How many cities are there in Northern Ireland?

a) five

b) two

c) seven

3 Puffins are a type of dog. True or not true?

a) true

b) not true

4 Which of these subjects does Jocelyn Bell Burnell study?

a) space

b) music

c) trees

5 People in Northern Ireland make a type of bread out of potato. True or not true?

a) true

b) not true

GLOSSARY

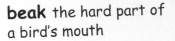

beak the hard part of a bird's mouth

bird of prey bird that hunts and kills other animals for food

black pudding black sausage that contains dried pig's blood

capital the city where the government (the group of people that leads a country) meets

cliff high, steep wall of rock

column tall, thin piece of rock

cricket sport in which players hit a ball with a bat and then run back and forth before the other team collects the ball

habitat type of natural area in which a plant or animal likes to live

hare animal that looks like a large rabbit with long ears

hockey game in which players use a long stick to try and hit a ball into a net at the other end of a field

international to do with two or more countries

jockey person who rides horses in races

lake large area of water that has land around it

lava hot, melted rock that comes out of a volcano

monument something that was built for a special person or event

mural large picture painted on a wall

otter animal with brown fur and a long body that lives in and around water

pasties small pies filled with chopped meat, fish and/or vegetables

president person who leads an organisation or a country

rock formation special shape or pattern that has been naturally formed by rock

seaweed plant that grows in the sea

shingle a shingle beach is made of small or medium-sized rounded stones

stew dish that is cooked slowly in a large pot and is often made with meat and vegetables

tourist person who is visiting a place for a holiday

traditional describes something that a group of people has done or made in the same way for a long time

volcano opening in the Earth's surface, around which a rocky hill has formed

INDEX

ANSWERS

Pages 5–21

Page 5: People think that part of the hill is the same shape as Napoleon Bonaparte's nose. Napoleon Bonaparte was the leader of France around 200 years ago.

Page 6: The other counties of Northern Ireland are: Antrim, Down, Fermanagh, Londonderry and Tyrone.

Page 8: There are 17 different types of butterfly living at White Park Bay. Four types are: Peacock, Small Copper, Orange Tip and Common Blue.

Page 11: There are many ships to choose from, but some famous ones built in Belfast are: HMS *Belfast*, RMS *Olympic*, HMHS *Britannic*, SS *Southern Cross* and SS *Canberra*.

Page 15: People think that Ballymacdermot Court Tomb was built between 4500 and 6000 years ago.

Page 16: Common seals and grey seals live in Strangford Lough.

Page 18: There are six other books set in Narnia: *Prince Caspian, The Voyage of the Dawn Treader, The Silver Chair, The Horse and His Boy, The Magician's Nephew* and *The Last Battle*.

Page 21: Hurling was first played around 3000 years ago.

Quiz answers

1	c)	4	a)
2	a)	5	a)
3	b)		

OTHER TITLES IN THE FACT CAT SERIES...

SPACE

THE EARTH
978 0 7502 8220 8

THE MOON
978 0 7502 8221 5

THE PLANETS
978 0 7502 8222 2

THE SUN
978 0 7502 8223 9

COUNTRIES

FRANCE
978 0 7502 8212 3

BRAZIL
978 0 7502 8213 0

GHANA
978 0 7502 8215 4

ITALY
978 0 7502 8214 7

WAYLAND